GEOLOGY
YOU CAN GOBBLE

JESSIE ALKIRE

Consulting Editor, Diane Craig, MA/Reading Specialist

Super Sandcastle

An Imprint of Abdo Publishing
abdobooks.com

ABDOBOOKS.COM

Published by Abdo Publishing, a division of ABDO, PO Box 398166, Minneapolis, Minnesota 55439. Copyright © 2019 by Abdo Consulting Group, Inc. International copyrights reserved in all countries. No part of this book may be reproduced in any form without written permission from the publisher. Super SandCastle™ is a trademark and logo of Abdo Publishing.

Printed in the United States of America, North Mankato, Minnesota
102018
012019

THIS BOOK CONTAINS RECYCLED MATERIALS

Design: Emily O'Malley, Mighty Media, Inc.
Production: Mighty Media, Inc.
Editor: Liz Salzmann
Cover Photographs: Mighty Media, Inc.; Shutterstock
Interior Photographs: Mighty Media, Inc.; Shutterstock; Wikimedia Commons

The following manufacturers/names appearing in this book are trademarks: Essential Everyday®, Haribo® Starmix™, Market Pantry™, Nestle®, PAM®, Pyrex®, Reynolds® Cut-Rite®, Starburst®, Target®

Library of Congress Control Number: 2018948860

Publisher's Cataloging-in-Publication Data
Names: Alkire, Jessie, author.
Title: Geology you can gobble / by Jessie Alkire.
Description: Minneapolis, Minnesota : Abdo Publishing, 2019 | Series: Super simple science you can snack on
Identifiers: ISBN 9781532117251 (lib. bdg.) | ISBN 9781532170119 (ebook)
Subjects: LCSH: Geology--Juvenile literature. | Cooking--Juvenile literature. | Science--Experiments--Juvenile literature. | Gastronomy--Juvenile literature.
Classification: DDC 641.0--dc23

Super SandCastle™ books are created by a team of professional educators, reading specialists, and content developers around five essential components—phonemic awareness, phonics, vocabulary, text comprehension, and fluency—to assist young readers as they develop reading skills and strategies and increase their general knowledge. All books are written, reviewed, and leveled for guided reading and early reading intervention programs for use in shared, guided, and independent reading and writing activities to support a balanced approach to literacy instruction.

TO ADULT HELPERS

The projects in this book are fun and simple. There are just a few things to remember to keep kids safe. Some projects require the use of hot objects. Also, kids may be using messy ingredients. Make sure they protect their clothes and work surfaces. Review the projects before starting, and be ready to assist when necessary.

KEY SYMBOLS

Watch for these warning symbols in this book. Here is what they mean.

HOT!
You will be working with something hot. Get help!

NUTS!
This snack includes nuts. Find out whether anyone you are serving has a nut allergy.

CONTENTS

WHAT IS GEOLOGY?

Geology is the study of Earth. Geologists study what Earth is made of. This includes rocks, **minerals**, landforms, and more. Studying these things helps geologists learn about Earth's history and how it might change in the future.

The history of geology goes back hundreds of years. Scottish scientist James Hutton studied rocks in the 1700s. Hutton came up with the rock **cycle**. This is a cycle through which Earth's rocks are formed, changed, and destroyed.

JAMES HUTTON

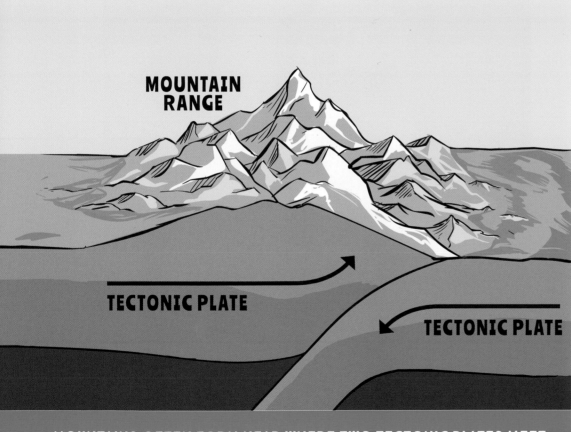

MOUNTAIN RANGE

TECTONIC PLATE

TECTONIC PLATE

MOUNTAINS OFTEN FORM NEAR WHERE TWO TECTONIC PLATES MEET.

In the 1960s, scientists discovered tectonic plates. These plates make up Earth's crust.

The tectonic plates move. This movement can cause mountains to form. Plate movement can also cause **earthquakes** and **volcanic** eruptions.

GEOLOGY TODAY

Today's geologists use many different tools and methods to study Earth. These include work in labs and using computers.

LAB WORK

Geologists study rocks, fossils, and **minerals** in labs. Scientists observe these objects with microscopes. They may use chemical tests to learn more about the objects.

GEOLOGISTS SORT ROCK SAMPLES IN LABS.

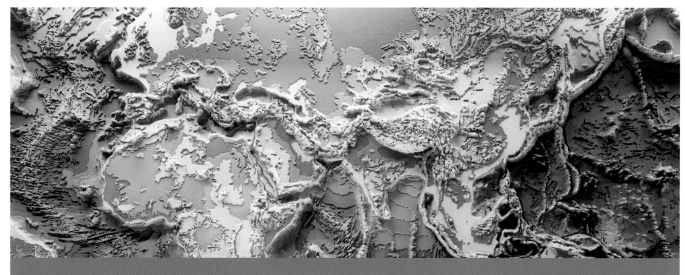

3-D PRINTERS CAN PRINT MAPS THAT SHOW EARTH'S LANDFORMS.

COMPUTER WORK

Geologists use computers to create geological maps for an area. These maps show the rocks and natural structures of the area.

Geologists also use computer programs to make models of rocks, **minerals**, landforms, and more. Geologists can use 3-D printers to create these models!

GEOLOGY SNACKS

You can learn a lot about geology by making the fun snacks in this book!

GET READY

* Ask an adult for **permission** to use kitchen tools and ingredients.

* Read the snack's list of tools and ingredients. Make sure you have everything you need.

* Does a snack require ingredients you don't like? Get creative! Find other ingredients you enjoy instead.

SNACK CLEAN & SAFE

* Clean your work surface before you start.

* Wash your hands before you work with food.

* Keep your work area tidy. This makes it easier to find what you need.

* Ask an adult for help when handling sharp or hot objects.

CLEANING UP

* Don't waste unused ingredients! Store leftover ingredients to use later.

* Clean your work surface. Wash any dishes or tools you used.

* Wash your hands before you eat your snack!

INGREDIENTS & TOOLS

BUTTERSCOTCH CHIPS

CHOCOLATE RICE CEREAL

CHOCOLATE SANDWICH COOKIES

CHOPPED WALNUTS

FOOD COLORING

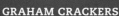

FRUITY RICE CEREAL

GRAHAM CRACKERS

GREEN SPRINKLES

GUMMY CANDIES

MINI MARSHMALLOWS

NON-STICK COOKING SPRAY

ROCK CANDY OF VARIOUS COLORS

SHREDDED COCONUT

STARBURST CANDIES

SWEETENED CONDENSED MILK

HERE ARE SOME OF THE INGREDIENTS AND TOOLS YOU WILL NEED TO MAKE THE SNACKS IN THIS BOOK.

ALUMINUM FOIL

BAKING SHEET

BOWLS

CANDY MOLD

CUTTING BOARD

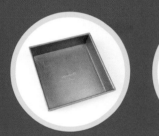

8 × 8-INCH BAKING PAN

HAMMER

MEASURING CUPS

MINI MUFFIN PAN

PLASTIC ZIPPER BAGS

PLATE

ROLLING PIN

SMALL, CLEAR PLASTIC CUPS

WAX PAPER

WHISK

TOOLS

PUDDING EARTH LAYERS

INGREDIENTS

- 2 small packages of instant vanilla pudding mix
- 1 small package of instant chocolate pudding mix
- milk
- chocolate sandwich cookies
- food coloring
- green sprinkles

TOOLS

- 2 large bowls
- measuring cup
- whisk
- gallon plastic zipper bag
- rolling pin
- 3 small bowls
- 4 spoons
- small, clear plastic cups

Earth has four layers. You can make a model of Earth's layers with pudding!

1. Pour both vanilla pudding mix packages into a large bowl. **Whisk** in 4 cups of milk.

2. Pour the chocolate pudding mix into the other large bowl. Whisk in 2 cups of milk.

3. Place both bowls of pudding in the refrigerator for 10 minutes.

4. Place 12 to 14 chocolate cookies in the plastic bag. Seal the bag. Roll a rolling pin over the bag to crush the cookies into **crumbs**. Set the bag aside.

5. Divide the vanilla pudding between the three small bowls.

6. Add several drops of orange food coloring to one bowl. Stir until the pudding turns orange.

7. Add several drops of red food coloring to the second bowl. Stir until the pudding turns red.

Continued on the next page.

11

12

13

8. Add several drops of yellow food coloring to the third bowl. Stir until the pudding turns yellow.

9. Put a couple spoonfuls of yellow pudding in a plastic cup. This represents Earth's inner **core**.

10. Add a couple spoonfuls of orange pudding to the cup. Don't mix the colors. The orange layer is Earth's outer core.

11. Add a couple spoonfuls of red pudding to the cup. This is Earth's mantle.

12. Add a couple spoonfuls of chocolate pudding. This is Earth's crust.

13. Top the crust with some crushed cookies and sprinkles. These are dirt and grass.

14. Repeat steps 9 through 13 with the rest of the pudding and cups. Then, share your Earth treat with friends!

SCIENCE BITE

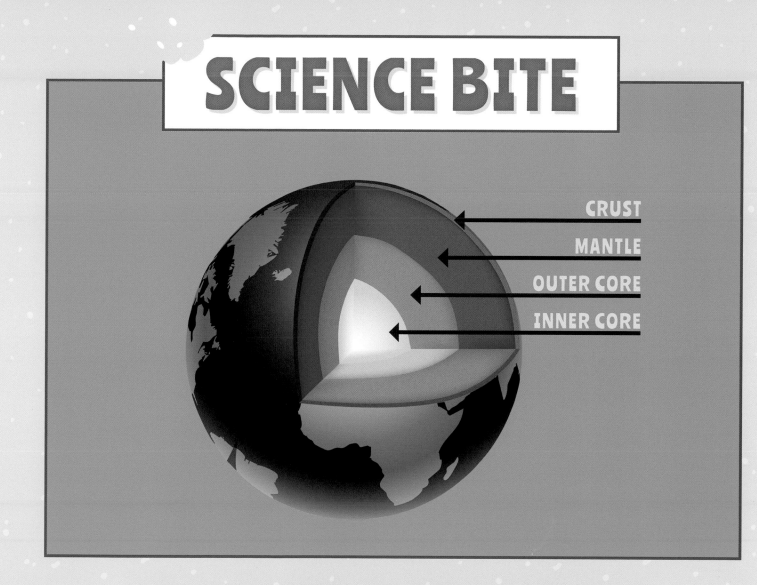

CRUST

MANTLE

OUTER CORE

INNER CORE

EARTH HAS FOUR LAYERS. THE INNER CORE IS THE CENTER OF EARTH. IT IS MADE OF SOLID IRON. THE OUTER CORE IS MOSTLY LIQUID IRON AND NICKEL. THE MANTLE IS MADE OF MAGMA. EARTH'S CRUST IS A THIN LAYER OF SOLID ROCK.

STARBURST ROCK CYCLE 🔥

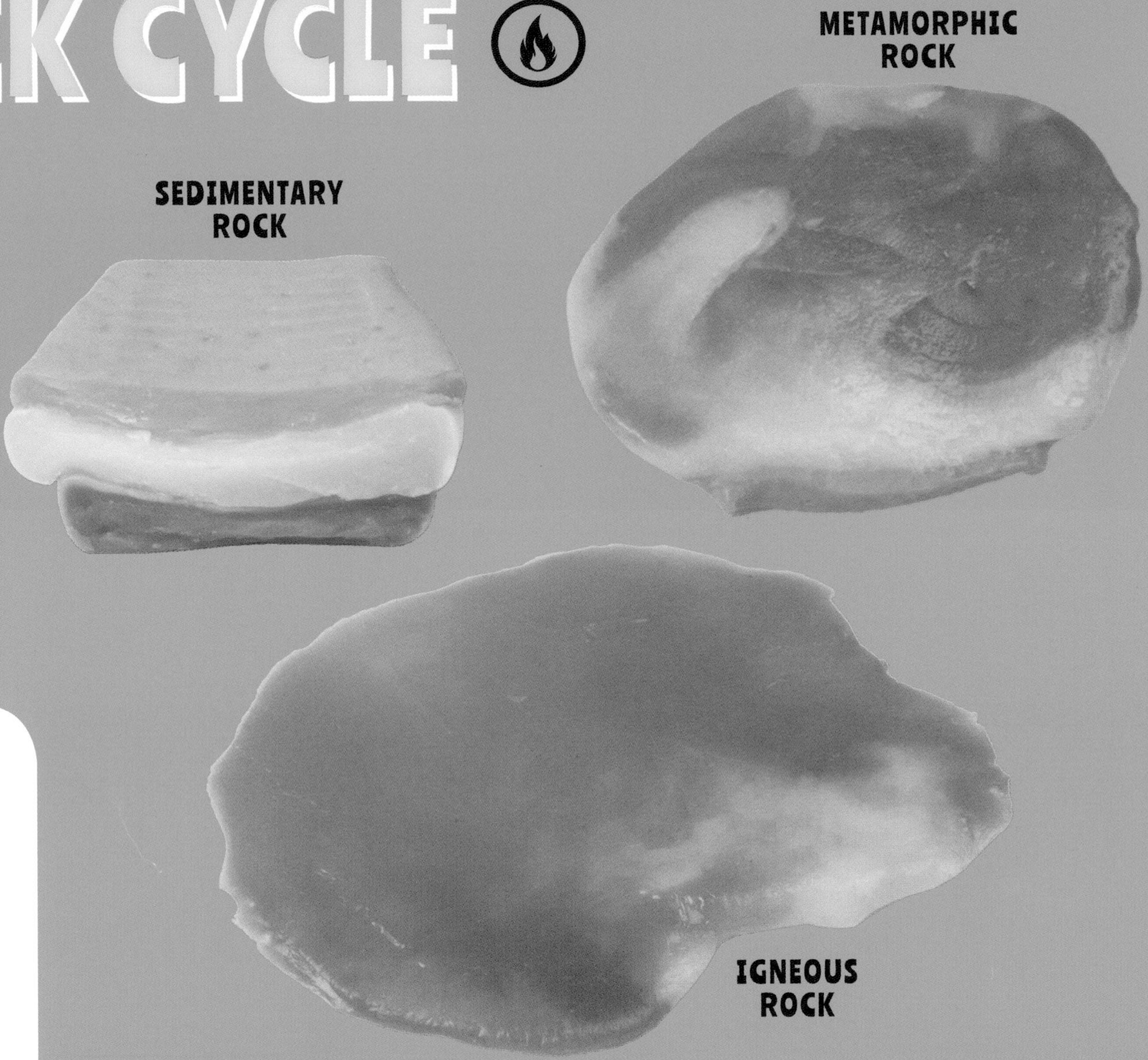

METAMORPHIC ROCK

SEDIMENTARY ROCK

IGNEOUS ROCK

INGREDIENTS

- 3 Starburst candies (different colors)

TOOLS

- plastic zipper bag
- wax paper

Rocks go through a **cycle** from sedimentary rock to metamorphic rock to igneous rock. These changes are caused by heat and pressure. You can recreate the rock cycle with Starburst candies!

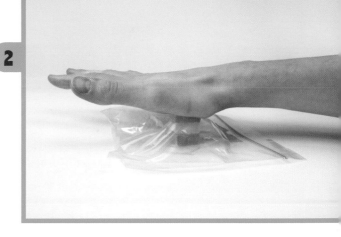

1. Unwrap three Starburst candies. These represent igneous rocks. Place the candies on top of each other inside the plastic bag.

2. Press down on the candies to compress them. The candies should form layers. This is sedimentary rock.

3. Place the compressed candies on a sheet of wax paper. Heat them in the microwave for 10 seconds. The candies should be soft but not melted. Let them cool for a few minutes.

4. Place the candies back in the plastic bag. Press down on the candies to compress them more. This is metamorphic rock.

5. Place the candies back on the wax paper. Heat them in the microwave for 30 seconds.

6. Let the candies cool completely and harden. This is igneous rock.

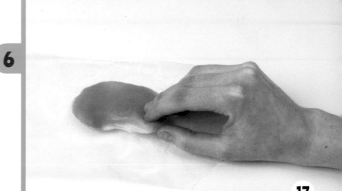

7. Make more Starburst rocks to share with your friends!

METAMORPHIC ROCK BARS 🔥 🥜

INGREDIENTS

- non-stick cooking spray
- ¼ cup butter
- 5 to 6 graham crackers
- ½ cup chocolate chips
- ½ cup butterscotch chips
- ½ cup chopped walnuts
- 1 cup sweetened condensed milk
- 1 cup shredded coconut

TOOLS

- 8 × 8 inch baking pan
- aluminum foil
- bowl
- oven mitts
- large plastic zipper bag
- rolling pin
- measuring cup
- spoon
- dinner knife

Metamorphic rock forms under Earth's surface where it is very hot. The heat and pressure change other types of rocks into metamorphic rocks. You can observe this change in a sweet treat!

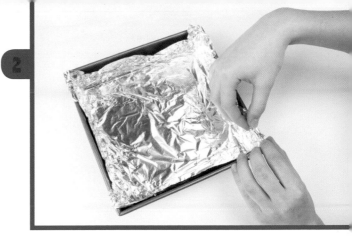

1. Preheat the oven to 350 **degrees** Fahrenheit.
2. Line the pan with aluminum foil. Spray the foil with cooking spray.
3. Place the butter in a bowl. Heat the butter in the microwave for 30 seconds. If it's not fully melted, microwave it for 30 more seconds.
4. Put five or six graham crackers in the plastic bag. Roll the rolling pin over the bag to crush the crackers into **crumbs**.

5. Add ¾ cup of graham cracker crumbs to the melted butter. Stir until the crumbs are coated with butter.
6. Press the graham cracker and butter mixture evenly into the pan.

Continued on the next page.

7. Sprinkle the chocolate chips over the graham cracker layer.

8. Sprinkle the butterscotch chips over the chocolate chips.

9. Sprinkle the chopped walnuts over the butterscotch chips.

10. Pour the sweetened condensed milk over everything.

11. Sprinkle the shredded coconut on top.

12. Bake the bars 20 to 25 minutes, or until brown.

13. Let the bars cool completely. Then, cut them into even squares.

14. Study your metamorphic rock bars. Can you see how the heat and pressure changed and combined the ingredients?

SCIENCE BITE

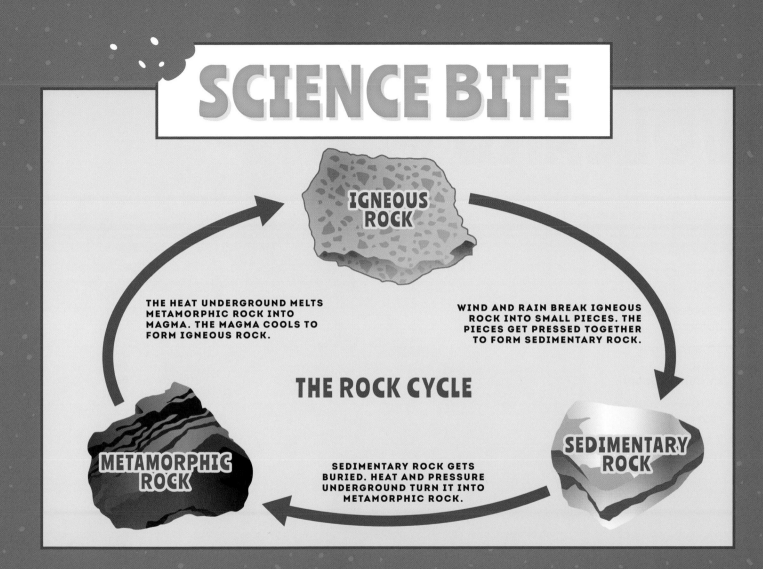

IGNEOUS ROCK

THE HEAT UNDERGROUND MELTS METAMORPHIC ROCK INTO MAGMA. THE MAGMA COOLS TO FORM IGNEOUS ROCK.

WIND AND RAIN BREAK IGNEOUS ROCK INTO SMALL PIECES. THE PIECES GET PRESSED TOGETHER TO FORM SEDIMENTARY ROCK.

THE ROCK CYCLE

METAMORPHIC ROCK

SEDIMENTARY ROCK GETS BURIED. HEAT AND PRESSURE UNDERGROUND TURN IT INTO METAMORPHIC ROCK.

SEDIMENTARY ROCK

THE SNACKS ON PAGES 16 THROUGH 20 ARE ABOUT THE ROCK CYCLE. THERE ARE THREE MAIN TYPES OF ROCKS. THESE ARE IGNEOUS ROCKS, SEDIMENTARY ROCKS, AND METAMORPHIC ROCKS. EACH KIND OF ROCK CAN TURN INTO ONE OF THE OTHER KINDS THROUGH THE ROCK CYCLE!

CRUNCHY CEREAL VOLCANO 🔥

INGREDIENTS

- non-stick cooking spray
- 4 tablespoons butter
- 10 ounce-bag mini marshmallows
- 5 cups chocolate rice cereal
- 1 to 2 cups fruity rice cereal

TOOLS

- large microwave-safe bowl
- oven mitts
- spoon
- wax paper
- baking sheet
- plate

Some geologists study **volcanoes**. Volcanoes are vents in Earth's crust. When they erupt, **lava**, ash, and rocks come out of the vent. You can make your own volcano with cereal and marshmallows!

1. Spray the bowl with cooking spray. Put the butter and marshmallows in the bowl.

2. Heat the bowl in the microwave for 30 seconds. Stir. Repeat until the marshmallow mixture is completely melted.

3. Gently stir the chocolate rice cereal into the marshmallow mixture.

4. Place wax paper on the baking sheet. Spray the wax paper with cooking spray.

5. Place the cereal mixture on the wax paper. With clean hands, gently press the cereal mixture into an even layer. Let it cool for 15 minutes.

6. Roll the cereal mixture into a cone. Place it on the plate. This is the volcano.

7. Fill the volcano with fruity rice cereal. Press some of the cereal into the side of the volcano to look like lava. Enjoy your crunchy cereal snack!

CHOCOLATE GEODES ⬤

INGREDIENTS

- 1 cup chocolate chips
- rock candy of various colors
- vanilla frosting

TOOLS

- microwave-safe bowl
- measuring cups
- oven mitts
- spoons
- circle or oval candy mold
- baking sheet
- plastic zipper bags
- cutting board
- hammer
- scissors

A geode is a hollow rock with colorful crystals inside. You can make your own **edible** geodes!

1. Put the chocolate chips in the bowl.

2. Heat the chocolate in the microwave for 30 seconds. Stir.

3. Repeat step 2 until the chocolate is fully melted.

4. Use a small spoon to spread a thin layer of chocolate into each section of the candy mold. Make sure each section is completely coated with an even layer of chocolate.

5. Set the mold on the baking sheet. Put it in the freezer for at least one hour.

6. Put one color of candy in a plastic bag. Seal the bag and set it on a cutting board. Crush the candy with a hammer.

7. Repeat step 6 for the remaining colors of candy.

Continued on the next page.

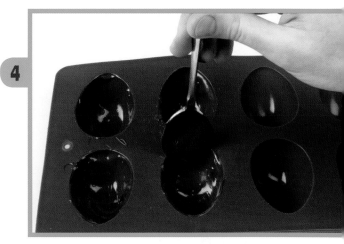

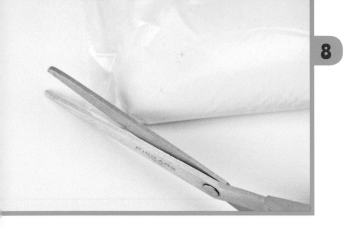

8

10

11

8. Put ¾ cup of frosting in another plastic bag. Seal the bag. Cut one corner of the bag to make a small hole.

9. Remove the candy mold from the freezer.

10. Gently **squeeze** the bag until frosting comes out of the hole. Use it to cover the chocolate in each section of the mold with frosting.

11. Sprinkle crushed candy on top of the frosting.

12. Put your candy geodes back in the freezer for one hour. Then, remove them from the mold. Enjoy your geode snacks!

SCIENCE BITE

GEODES OFTEN FORM FROM VOLCANIC ROCKS. THE PROCESS TAKES THOUSANDS OF YEARS. FIRST, AIR BUBBLES FORM IN LAVA. THE LAVA COOLS TO FORM A ROCK. THE AIR BUBBLES ARE TRAPPED IN THE LAVA ROCK. THIS CREATES A SPACE INSIDE THE ROCK. WATER FILLS THIS SPACE. MINERALS FROM THE WATER GET LEFT BEHIND IN THE SPACE. THEN THE MINERALS GROW INTO COLORFUL CRYSTALS!

JELL-O AMBER FOSSILS ⬤

INGREDIENTS

- orange, apricot, peach, or mango Jell-O mix
- 2 cups water
- non-stick cooking spray
- gummy candies

TOOLS

- measuring cups
- large bowl
- spoon
- mini muffin pan

Fossils are the preserved remains of dead plants and animals. Fossils can be in rock or amber. Amber is hardened tree **resin**. You can make your own amber fossils with Jell-O!

1. Have an adult help you boil 1 cup of water. Pour the water into a large bowl. Stir in the Jell-O until the powder **dissolves** completely.

2. Add 1 cup of cold water to the Jell-O mixture.

3. Spray each muffin cup with cooking spray. Fill each cup three-quarters full with Jell-O mixture. Save some Jell-O mixture for later.

4. Put the muffin pan in the refrigerator for 15 minutes.

5. Take the muffin pan out of the refrigerator. Press a gummy candy into each cup.

6. Add more Jell-O mixture to each muffin cup.

7. Put the muffin pan back in the refrigerator for several hours. Then remove the amber fossils from the muffin pan.

CONCLUSION

Geology is the study of Earth, what it's made of, and its processes. Geologists try to learn about Earth's structure and history and how it has changed over time.

MAKING SNACKS IS JUST ONE WAY TO LEARN ABOUT GEOLOGY. HOW WILL YOU CONTINUE YOUR GEOLOGY ADVENTURE?

QUIZ

1 | **GEOLOGY IS THE STUDY OF WEATHER.** TRUE OR FALSE?

2 | **HOW MANY LAYERS DOES EARTH HAVE?**

3 | **WHAT KIND OF ROCK HAS COLORFUL CRYSTALS INSIDE IT?**

LEARN MORE ABOUT IT!

YOU CAN FIND OUT MORE ABOUT GEOLOGY AT THE LIBRARY. OR YOU CAN ASK AN ADULT TO HELP YOU FIND INFORMATION ABOUT GEOLOGY ON THE INTERNET!

ANSWERS: 1. FALSE 2. FOUR 3. A GEODE

GLOSSARY

core – the center of a space object such as a planet, moon, or star.

crumb – a tiny piece of something, especially food.

cycle – a series of events that happen over and over again.

degree – the unit used to measure temperature.

dissolve – to mix with a liquid so that it becomes part of the liquid.

earthquake – when the ground shakes or trembles.

edible – safe to eat.

lava – hot, melted rock from inside a volcano.

magma – melted rock below Earth's surface.

mineral – a naturally occurring, solid substance that is not animal or vegetable, such as gold, ore, and some stones.

permission – when a person in charge says it's okay to do something.

resin – a sticky, translucent, yellow or brown substance that comes from certain trees.

squeeze – to press the sides of something together.

volcano – a deep opening in Earth's surface from which hot liquid rock or steam comes out. Something related to volcanoes is volcanic.

whisk – to stir something quickly with a whisk or a fork.